We Share The Road

We Share The Road

Poems

For Seasons of the Year
and of the Soul

Lawrence H. Janssen
Illustrated by Betty B. Janssen

The Cedars Press
Green Lake, Wisconsin

Illustrated by Betty B. Janssen
Cover Photo: "Cliff Road In Winter" (American Baptist
        Assembly, Green Lake, WI) by Lawrence H. Janssen
Printing by Ripon Community Printers, Ripon, WI

Library of Congress Catalog Card Number preassigned is: 89-81992

ISBN: 0-917575-06-7

Published by The Cedars Press, Green Lake, WI

Printed and Bound in the United States of America

TABLE OF CONTENTS

SUMMER

AUTUMN

SEASONS OF THE SOUL

We Share The Road

The title poem pretty much sums up the philosophy by which I try to live. All that I own, all that sustains me, all that I am permitted to enjoy is a gift to be shared with other human beings and with all created things. I am an ecologist because the universe is ecological. There is but one "household" and I am but a single sharer in it. I am part of a living web in which all things are so intricately intertwined that I can never extricate myself from it. Nor should I wish to do so, for without those relationships, my life would not only be diminished, it would be impossible.

I am blest by what has come to me from the past. I am an inheritor of countless generations who, through eons of time, have been sharers like myself. And all future generations will be blest by what I pass on to them. They are my heirs. My task is so to steward my inheritance that their life will be possible, and that it will be good. To the degree to which I am faithful to the trust given me, through preservation, conservation and restoration of the air I breathe, the water I drink, the materials I use, and the beauty I enjoy, I will fulfill my stewardship on earth. To the degree that I waste, destroy or use more than I need, I break faith with all of life yet to come.

Life is not only ecological. It is theological. To speak of stewardship is to speak of accountability to a higher power. To speak of gifts is to acknowledge a giver. That giver, that higher power, is God. It is to God that I owe my ultimate stewardship. I exercise that stewardship by the manner in which I share the road. My lifestyle is my only witness in the courts of justice that will one day require me to account for my life on earth.

In committing these poems to print it is my prayer that I might have some small part in expanding in others an awareness of the meaning of having been made in the image of God, and of sharing "dominion."

Lawrence H. Janssen
Green Lake, Wisconsin
November 1989.

Introduction

The poems in this book have grown over a span of nearly twenty years. Their essence is a distillation of experiences and emerging concepts of what it means to be a faithful steward of God's world. They derive from a lifetime of awareness of how fragile is the web of life on the one hand, and how persistently benevolent is the will of God on the other.

POEMS FOR SEASONS OF THE YEAR grew out of the experiences described, many of them at the American Baptist Assembly, Green Lake, Wisconsin. They are word pictures, often without a pointed lesson. Yet each has within it the substance of the faith that has been growing within me until now. If some seem a bit whimsical, consider that life has its whimsical side; and even whimsy is not without meaning. Also, consider how the word "seasons" implies a rhythm which is basic to life. As we flow with the rhythms of seasons and of the vaster movements of the universe, we are sustained and enriched by them. We are part of the flow of life that began with creation and which will endure to the end of time.

In POEMS FOR SEASONS OF THE SOUL will be found a miscellany of thoughts that have come at questing times in my life. Some reveal moments of joyous revelation, some are written in appreciation of a special friend. And at least one, *Kid Gloves and No Socks,* recalls a memory of childhood in which my grandmother described the village snob, who tried to impress but didn't get by with the children. It, too, has deep meaning.

Special thanks are due to Betty Janssen for the drawings which enhance these pages. In addition:

To those who have encouraged me

to commit these poems to a book,

my heartfelt thanks.

To those who have inspired their writing,

or in other ways shared the road,

these poems are dedicated.--lhj

14

Seasons

of the

Year

WINTER

It's winter now and fallen snow

Drapes the hills and shrouds the trees,

And loveliness in crystal form

Encases stalk, and twigs, and leaves.

WE SHARE THE ROAD

Two young deer pause in the road--
    their hair ruffed against the cold,
    watching as my feet
    make tracks across new snow
    and send the squeaking sound of
       boots on frozen crystal
    against the wall and
      echoing through the trees.

Are these the same, who, as weeks-old fawns
    tripped so lightly one day last spring,
    their hooves clicking on the pavement,
    their dappled sides alight with sun,
    and leaped away when my presence
      was betrayed?

Now in the deep of winter, we share again the road,
   the same need for shelter from the cold,
      and food to keep the body warm.

And they, grown more alert,
   sense my presence long before I know of theirs.

They choose to stand and watch,
   and I to go quietly and in awe,
   lest this world of beauty
   be diminished one iota by some fear
      I caused to grow
   in lovely creature, with whom
   God has given me to share the road.

WINTER TIME ILLUSION

I shovelled a path across the lawn
    Where the flagstones show in summer,
And found beneath the crusted snow
    A maze of roads and tunnels
Where hungry voles in search of food
    From their burrows beneath the wall,
Crisscrossed the yard trying to find
    The seeds they missed last fall.

Though winter grips the earth with cold,
I come to this conclusion:
    That all things sleep beneath the snow
    Is winter time illusion.

CHICKADEE

Little bird in formal dress
    calling from the linden tree,
    you coax me out to offer food,
    appealing to the child in me.

Perching on my outstretched hand,
    you are so very small;
    I feel you clutch my fingertips,
    but sense no weight at all.

Little bird, you take me back
    to Eden where it all began,
    where God created polliwogs,
    and chickadees, and MAN.

Your simple trust restores the faith
    I've clung to all along;
    we're made for peace and harmony,
    and lives of joy and song.

AVALANCHE OF SNOW

All through the night
 the crystal snow
  drifted down
 until at dawn the tree tops bowed
  and branches bent,
   burdened to the ground.

And still it fell,
 as flake by flake
  its masses grew;
 Nor woodland creature stirred to mar
  its dimpled surface
   on the ground.

And then a breeze
 began to stir
  the laden trees until,
 dislodged, the snow
  went avalanching down
   and upward plumed
  in clouds of crystal.

TONIGHT NO SHADOW

Tonight there is no silhouette
    Across the golden moon,
    No naked branch against the sky,
Across the snow no shadowed form
    Along the garden path.

Five years ago the great oak tree,
    Of sixty summers past,
    Since acorn fell 'mid autumn leaves,
Gave up its green and never donned
    The signs of life again.

Then flickers came and beat for grubs
    Beneath its furrowed bark,
    And song birds sang their mating songs,
While chipmunks scurried to their lairs
    Beneath its aging bole.

Today when saw bit rotting bark
    And found the solid wood,
    Rending trunk from rooted stump,
It fell without a cry, its height
    Full measured on the ground.

And now I sit before the fire,
    Warmed by the slow release
    Of sixty years of morning dew
And summer days and setting suns
    And moonlit winter nights.

24

INTERDEPENDENCE

In the night the restless water of the lake
    surrendered to relentless cold,
    and, with autumnal overturn complete,
    became imprisoned to a glaze of ice--
        prisoner to itself in different form,

So silently that ducks, asleep,
    missed the change
        to crystal immobility;
And, with heads beneath their wings,
    were frozen in,
    helpless and without hope,
    until their plight was known
        to those still free.

These, huddling round,
    responding to some primal urge,
    defied the grip of ice,
    gave of their bodies' warmth,
        and thawed them free.

WHERE FOOTPRINTS MINGLE

The tracks I made on woodland path
    at evening in new fallen snow
    were there at dawn when dusky woods
    began to light with sun's first glow.

But now the tracks, there intertwined,
    of rabbit, squirrel and deer
    who came and went in nighttime hours
    betray the presence here
        of other creatures, small and large,
        who share the path I go
        in search of nature's peaceful calm
    through footprints mingled in the snow.

WHERE WING TIPS ETCHED THE SNOW

I went for a tramp one winter morn
    When dawn first grayed the sky,
Across the field and through the woods
    Where the great oaks lifted high
Their rugged boles and lofty crowns
    In casual symmetry
Above the path on which I trod
    To form a canopy.

The virgin snow lay undisturbed
    Where flake by flake it fell;
No track had marred its crystal breast,
    No sign was there to tell
Of woodland creature seeking food;
    And silence everywhere
Hung draped from weed and bush and tree
    And filled the frosty air.

Then by the trail I read this tale,
    A drama old as time:
A rabbit slept beneath the snow,
    Half camouflaged by rime;
A great horned owl on downy wings,
    And silently as night,
Swooped close to earth to claim its prey
    And raised again in flight.

I ponder still this mystery,
    As day by day I go,
That life gave life by way of death
    Where wing tips etched the snow.

ALEUT BOY

His words were few,
      but as he stood
      on the steep edge
      of a frozen pond
he skipped a stone
      on steel-hard ice
      and taught me that
      the ice could sing.

      And later on
            near glacier's edge,
            where trees draped down
            with clinging snow,
      he touched a bough
            and snowy wheels
            cascaded down
            to vale below.

MAPLE NECTAR

When snow softens in the drifts,

and frosty nights pursue

ever warming days,

When sap rises to meet beckoning spring,

pails hung on maples promise

distilled nectar later on.

SPRING

SPRING needs no ringing of a bell

To announce its coming.

In the opening of a flower

The softened air grows sweet

And SPRING is here!

WHEN MARCH STRUTS OUT

When March struts out on center stage,
    To take the place of mastery,
And elements of Winter wage
    Their battle for supremacy
And lose, and Spring becomes the star,
    As waking nature dons the garb
Of springtime green across the grass,
    And fragrant springtime odors pass
On every breeze that gently blows
    To ruffle nature's new-grown clothes;

Then tree sap rises from the roots,
    Drawing nurture from the ground,
Through trunk and branch to the very tip
    Of each small twig until it's found
The waiting buds of leaf and flower
    That soon will form a springtime bower,
A canopy of cooling shade
    Above the lane where lad and maid
Will stroll along, and hand in hand
    Exchange with joy their summer plans;

Then song birds migrate from the south
    And search for food they left last fall,
Declare their love in mating songs,
    And build their nests in orchard boughs;
Then through the drifts of fallen leaves
    Push pointed spikes of greening sheaves
From bulbs that slept the winter through,
    And violets color green grass blue,
And springtime gladness is the rage
    When March struts out on center stage.

IN HUMBLE AWE

I have tramped the fields and woods
    in search of flowers whose blooms
  would take me back to other times
    and places when my heart was young,
  and eager mind would race with questions
    of how such beauty could unfold
    from damp brown earth a thing
        as lovely as arbutus,
        or lady's slipper, softly pink
        or yellow stained with red.

Sometimes the sought for quarry has eluded me,
    the season being not just right,
  or the illusive flower lost
    through thoughtless plunderer who
    cherished vased-bloom more than
      in native habitat.

But when my quest has found its goal,
    as rare as painted trillium
    or common as forget-me-nots,
  My mind is stirred to marvel at a God
    whose creative love has filled the earth
    with varied wonder,
      and oft I kneel in humble awe.

IN MUTED TONES

Spring does not come on certain date
    when sun has reached a latitude
    that wise men say marks the change
    from winter gray to gayer mood.

In the air a whisper of wings,
    the far-off call of geese in flight,
    the sibilant sound of waxwings come
    from winter sojourn in the night.

The snowdrop spikes of white and green
    that push their way through matted leaves,
    the maple buds that swell on twigs
    with sap that rises in the trees,

The redenning osiers in the swamp,
    and catkins soft as down on wings,
    report the news in muted tones
    reserved for those who take note of spring.

TIME OF SINGING

All winter long sparrows
    searched the snow,
        gleaning seeds spilled by other birds
        from the feeder shelf,
    their scratching interspersed
        with cheeps and chirps
        that scarcely made a song--
a complement to nasal sound
        of nuthatch searching upside down
        for insects under bark--
        and call of chickadee, or
        flicker cries from deep
            within the woods.

It there were songs of grosbeak,
    junco, titmouse, finch,
        I missed them in the silence
        of the snow.

Then on a day when snowdrifts
    sagged beneath the sun
        in tired contours by the path,
        and buds were swelling on the trees,
the cheery song of cardinal
        pierced the winter air.
The time of singing had come again.

THE FLOWERS KNOW

When winter lasts too long
    and snow has lost its charm,
    and ice still grips the lake
    and nights are cold and clear,
I weary of waiting for winter's end.

Then snowdrops push their way through drifts,
    and scillas bloom where lawn is bare
    and bloodroot joins the wakening throng;
    and I rejoice, for one things' clear,
The flowers know it's spring.

SPRINGTIME MEDLEY

Night comes, and the whole earth sleeps;
    but not all, for fireflies
    blink on and off at the garden's edge;
And bats, in zig-zag course
    gobble insects on the wing.
Great horned owls in silent flight
    make shadows in the moonlight.
And a whip-poor-will, from the far wood's edge,
    calls the whole night through, and when
    the plaintive song has died
    on the still dawn air, as light begins to show
    where last the sun arose,
A cardinal in crimson coat
    begins to sound
    his whistled note until
    from far-off perch
    an answer comes in dialogue.

Then sparrows in the hedgerows twitter
      as though to tune
      their voices for the day, and then
      sound forth in cheeps and trills as if
      not to sing would cause their lungs to burst.

And field and forest come alive
      with songs of jay and thrush and oriole,
      catbirds, thrashers, vereos,
      and mourning doves and crows,
      and grosbeaks, robins, and birds
I do not know, until at last
      the tiny wren joins in
      the medley of song.

I LOVE THE STARS

I love the stars --
    especially on those nights
    when no moon cancels out
        the points of light that reach
        across the dark abyss.

'Tis then I walk alone,
    content to feel the vastness
    that surrounds and sense
        affinity with all that was
        and yet will be.

A moonlight walk is good
    for when I need to see
    the subtle outline of a trail
        or encroaching bush or tree;
But stars were made for walks
    when feet know well the path
    and mind is freed to contemplate
        how stars each night return
        and constant in the heavens burn,
            oblivious to the cares of earth.

While science probes with monumental force
    the secrets of the universe,
    beneath the stars my questing heart
        knows peace, and in my soul I sing
        for mysteries I cannot comprehend.

FAIRY RINGS

A fairy ring is not a fairy ring at all,
But ring of toadstools or Indian pipes,
Where rotting stump or old dead fall
of forest giant has prepared
a feast for saprophytic plants
that spring up overnight
and vanish in a day,
And thus complete the cycle,
centuries long,
That spells the tale of life on earth
since dawn.

A fairy ring is not a fairy ring at all.
And yet, if fairies are the embodiment
of life and death and all
The mysteries that lie between,
from where life ends
and whence it springs,
Then I believe they're fairy rings.

MORNING IN SPRING

It was the time of year when
  the slightest breeze sent
    showers of apple blossoms
    drifting to the grass.

Robins, awake before the sun,
  called to each other in the
    morning twilight, and

Rabbits nibbled clover before
  skittering off to cover
    in the hedgerows, where
      young were nested against
      the cold of vernal night.

Slowly the rising sun made
  silhouette of all the east horizon,
  slanting rays probed the shadows,
    and day broke, silently, but
  with decisiveness that denied repeal.

LOON MYSTERY

For sixty million years the loon
    has bred on northern inland lakes,
Despising land, except where edges
    hide a nest among the sedges.

And still the loon's primeval cry
    disturbs the night and pre-dawn air
with haunting songs, as at their birth,
    'ere human kind set foot on earth.

And resting on far-distant seas,
    their wintry migratory home,
Afloat throughout both nights and days,
    they hide the secrets of their ways.

Time distant creature of the wild,
    you wake in me creation's joy,
Far-reaching back to days of old,
    lost in the mysteries you hold.

SUMMER

Now summer's here and languid days

    Cause earth to teem with growing things,

As gardens, fields, and orchard trees

    Foretell the store that harvest brings.

AT SUNRISE

Across the fields of hay and corn,
 Whose hedgerows check the land,
The morning fog lies fencepost deep,
 While here and there a strand,
A wisp of vagrant cloud drifts up
 Like smoke gone out of hand.

The eastern glow of rising sun
 Betrays the infant day,
And color spreads in pastel hues
 From sun's reflected rays,
As probing fingers pierce the lace
 That hems the world with gray.

A jay calls from the ancient oak,
    A raucous sort of sound,
A pheasant cock begins to crow
    From somewhere on the ground.
God's sleeping world begins to wake
    To splendor all around.

And soon all things that crawl or creep,
    Or fly or walk the earth,
Feel quickening of the pulse of life,
    As day starts giving birth,
Rejoicing in their creaturehood,
    And God who gives them worth.

SUNRISE -- SUNSET

The sunset tells of coming night,
  With multi-colored rays
Spread across the darkening sky
  At parting of the day.

It fills with awe the wondering soul
  At mysteries of light
That show such splendor as the day
  Fades away to night.

Yet flaming sunrise often vies
  With sunset's many hues
From prismic spread of broken light
  In cloud and mist and dew;

And sometimes eastern skies light up
  When west is all aglow
With sun's last rays, as if to say,
  You shan't have all the show.

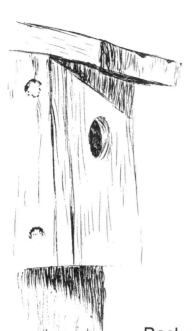

BLUEBIRD

Back and forth, forth and back,

    she flits from tree to hedge,

Each time a wisp of grass,

    neglected by last year's mower,

Deftly enlaced in cradle form

    for eggs that reflect the sky,

And infant nestlings

    to sing another spring.

SUMMER STARS

I don't know the way of stars,
    I call but few by their own name,
But this I know, from what I've seen
    Summer stars are not the same.
    They're not the same as those that shine
    In spring or fall or wintertime.

Oh, I know the points of light
    That leap to press the ceaseless chase
Across the chasms of the sky
    And mark their paths through trackless space,
    Remain the same the whole year through,
    And constant burn in night sky's blue.

Winter stars are sharp and cold,
　　Sparkling points of icy light;
And springtime stars are soft as dew
　　　And share the smell of springtime nights;
　　　And autumn stars are red and gold,
　　　Mellow with haze of a year grown old.

But summer stars are friendly stars
　　That glimmer out when day is done;
Summer stars are soothing stars
　　　That bring relief from burning sun;
　　　Summer stars, in a special way,
　　　Bring me rest at close of day.

Oh, you may know the way of stars,
　　And call each one by its own name,
And contradict, but I aver
　　　That summer stars are not the same.

FIREFLIES

From overhead the stars look down
     benignly on a darkened world;
The dipper's there, and Arcturus,
     Orion, Pegasus and Mars.

But as I walked a meadow path
     When dew was forming on the grass,
The blinking lights of fireflies
     Appeared to rival light of stars.

When I'm o'erwhelmed by science lore,
     Of magnitude and speed of light,
I give my thoughts to simple things
     Like fireflies on a summer night.

I NEVER WALK THE SHORE

I never walk the shore
but pockets bulge
with polished stones
and sculptured wood
and broken shells
culled from wave-tossed
heaps of sand.
No matter that later on
I'll wonder what I saw
of beauty in their form;
I never walk the shore
but pockets bulge.

MYSTERIES OF NIGHT

The rising sun in daily round
    pulls back the coverlet of night
    and draws the populace from sleep
       in slow progression 'round the world,

To a day of awe inspiring wonder
    and mysteries at which to be amazed
    because to comprehend is beyond
       the power of the mind.

And when the sun, its splendor spent,
    draws again the coverlet of dark,
    it tucks them in like children
       trundled off to bed --
    for some, to sleep, while others probe
       the mysteries of night.

THE NEXT CROP

For a hundred years the land had known
    The plow's keen blade and disc's sharp edge,
Rending the roots of last year's crop,
    Turning the furrow 'twixt woods and sedge
    Where wetland marked the end of soil
    Fit to reward the farmer's toil.

One hundred years of hay and corn,
    Of oats and beans, and wheat and rye,
And oxen plodding in the furrow--
    Six inches deep, straight as a die--
    And then the plow by horses drawn,
    Followed by tractor later on.

Three generations tilled the land,
    Plowed and planted the sandy loam,
The father, son, and his son's son
    Had claimed the homestead as their own,
    Heard the plowshare's whispered sound
    And smelled the smell of new turned ground.

But now the land for ten years past
    Has rested from its yearly toil,
And from the edge the trees creep in
    To fight for nurture from the soil,
    As seeds the winds and birds have dropped
    Contrive to form the field's next crop.

VESPER PRAYER

Across the land at evening
    The shadows lengthen
        As the day fades away to night.

And all the wonders of the
        sunlit hours
    Take on new mystery
      As stars appear
And night sounds come drifting
      on the breeze.

Lord, draw near to me--
    And draw me near--
That thou my pulsing heart
    Might still . . .
      And quiet, I might go to rest.

BENEDICTION

The last rays of sun
      touched the treetops
            like a benediction.

The breeze caressed the land
      as a mother her children
            when she tucks them into bed.

The growing dark brought out
      the evening star
            low on the west horizon,

and the rising moon above
      the eastern hills
            bathed the earth with magic.

AUTUMN

The bright blue days of autumn

Bring night times crisp and cold.

The verdant scenes of summer

Are burnished now with gold.

WHEN COLOR RIOTS

I saw the first red leaf today,
High on the tree and tucked away
Amid the maple's summer green,
As if reluctant to be seen,
To be accused of harbinging
The brilliant reign of autumn's fling,
And through some act contrariwise
To hasten summer's sure demise.

But seen or not, the change will come,
And reluctant Summer will succumb
To cooler nights and mellow days,
And lower slant of sun's bright rays;
And squirrels will hoard the hickory crop,
And grapes turn purple in the copse;
And autumn's advent will be known
When wild geese go winging home.

The annual race cannot be stayed;
Nor can the worth of each be weighed
Against the other, claiming best
One season's good above the rest.
Summer, winter, spring and fall,
Have their merit, each and all,
And I rejoice in autumn's moods,
When color riots in the woods.

AWAITING SPRING

There's a glory in the woods
where leaves of burnished gold
and shades of flaming crimson
adorn the maple, hickory and oak.

And soon, with autumn's flourish past,
they'll loose their fragile hold
and fall rustling to the ground.

But on each twig where now they cling
new buds await the bursting
of protective scales
when summoned forth by spring.

A FEATHER IN THE SAND

I walked the shore
      and just ahead
a yearling gull
      by leaps and glides
kept pace as if
      perchance to coax
through mews and cries
      some tidbit from my empty hand.

      Till tired at last
          of fruitless game
   with one last cry
      she took to wing,
   soared low above
      the wind-tossed waves
   then circled back
      and dropped a feather in the sand.

TREES LEAVE NO SCAR

Trees are for bending before the wind
    or gently swaying in the breeze;
      For standing strong under ice and snow
          all winter long,
      And spreading leafy boughs and
          fragrant blossoms in the spring.

Trees are for growing wood and cooling shade,
    For bird homes in their branches
        and picnics on the ground.

Trees are for yielding fruit and nuts in season,
    And giving of their summer leaves
    To spread protective blanket for
        next year's springtime flowers,
        or make rich soil for seasons yet to come.

Trees are for lifting high or spreading wide
    All the distilled loveliness
            of sun and rain,
    The transformed fury of the storms of wind
            and hail and sleet and snow.

Trees are for standing in one place
    Generation after generation,
Landmarks of a trail,
    Reminders of joyous times and sad.

Trees leave no trace of silhouette
           when they are gone,
No scar against the sky
           to show where they have been--

But in the ground are root and stump
    from which new shoots may grow,
    or seeds to reproduce
           each one its kind.

FIRST FIRE OF FALL

The match flame transfers to paper and wood,
    curling smoke, then licking flames,
And I am off in reverie
    of sun and rain that formed
    of earth where seed had dropped
    an infant tree that grew
        to sapling and then
        a towering pillar in the forest--

Storage place for sunsets and rises
    and starry nights and moon bathed hours,
And winter times when naked limbs
    bore fury of the storm
    or lay bedecked in snow
    while slanting rays of sun
        caught and prismed back
        colors of the rainbow.

THE HICKORY CROP

Throughout the night the falling nuts
    rattled from the hickory trees,
    loosed by frost and shaken free
      by autumn's intermittent breeze.

When rooster crowed at dawn's first light
    before the sun traversed the space
    where sky and earth pretend to meet
      I rose from interrupted sleep

and ventured forth with mittened hands
    against October's morning chill
    to gather up the fallen fruit,
      but found no trace of where it fell;

For early squirrels had sallied forth
    before the day had come awake
    to store away the hickory crop
      I'd hoped would flavor Christmas cakes.

Nor did I in the least complain,
    for squirrels are part of what I need
    to integrate my woodland plot
      with larger nature's wild domain.

INDIAN SUMMER

The days had crept to the edge of winter
    Along the path where autumn draped
In reds and golds and rusty hues
    Her multi-colored shawl of lace.

Each night the rime bejewelled the grass
    As if by touch of fairy wand,
And air turned chill with hint of snow,
    And icy crystals etched the pond.

The summer crops were laid in store
    In burdened granary and mow,
And orchard fruits were gathered in,
    And stubble yielded to the plow.

Blossoms in the wayside grass
    Hung limp and drab on withered stalk,
No longer host to droning bee,
    No longer gracing garden walk.

The birds whose echoed mating songs
    Rang from orchard boughs last spring,
And wild geese in wavy skeins
    Had emptied sky of migrant wings.

Then in the night a shift of wind
    Swept winter breath from frosty air,
As Indian Summer claimed her day,
    And nights were warm and days were fair.

HOPE OF SPRINGTIME

I walked 'mid autumn's splendor,
    Shuffling through the leaves,
The fading golds and crimson
    Fallen from the trees.

I saw the children playing,
    Catching leaves in air;
Of the dying season,
    Naively unaware.

While I with great reluctance
    Let go the passing days,
They read the hope of springtime
    In October's golden haze.

LEAVES OF IVY

For days the Boston ivy burned
    With autumnal flame
Against the wall of glacial stone
    Where clinging tendrils bound
Its lattice work of twisting stems
    To alien boulders found
When breaking plow split the sod
    Exposing fertile ground.

Then in the night condensing fog
    Dripped in icy lace
From each leaf's edge a crystal weight
    That tore the slender threads
By which, through days of summer green
    The growing plant was fed,
Till leaves and shattered crystal lay
    Along the stone wall's ledge.

Now with autumn's harvest in,
    of apples, wheat and rye,
And memory stored up to the brim
    With images of fall,
Musing by the winter fire,
    Things of beauty I recall:
Frost filled air, geese winging home,
    And leaves of ivy on the wall.

POSTLUDE

Again cold winter's ice and snow
 Enshroud each twig and blade,
And 'cross the fields in fluffy folds
 Is like a blanket laid.

The teeming earth has gone to sleep,
 Its straining days of toil are done.
The time of harvest now is past,
 The time for peaceful rest has come.

Praise God who makes the earth rejoice,
 Praise God who makes the seasons run
And gives us succor through the year,
 From sun to snow, from snow to sun.

Seasons

of the

Soul

WE WRITE THE SONG

Life can be a cacophony of sound,
    or a song;
A nerve jarring jangle,
     or a harmony
       that soothes or stirs to action,
       that speaks of peace and joy,
         or sadness and despair.

We sort and cull and rearrange
    to make the song
    with which our lives
    identify.

The sounds are given.
    We write the song!
    We write the song!

TO HELP THE HEART REMEMBER

Vision fades and memories
are overlaid with time that dims
the love and joy
that fed our souls along the way
we came to what we are.

And so we gather relics of the past,
and in diaries record
the journey of our days --
and photographs of cherished things
to help the heart remember.

REMEMBERED SMILES

Before words, smiles were the language
    that conveyed
   the messages that passed
    from soul to soul--
  messages that inspired
    and affirmed;
  that welded two in friendship's bond,
   and in the bonds of love.

And smiles that brighten eyes
    and upward curve the lips
  still speak a symphony of meaning
    in themes too lofty and too deep
    for uttered words.

Long after they are spoken and the sounds
   of words are gone,
 in times of loneliness or need,
 I think your name and hear
   the music of remembered smiles.

MEMORY IS AN ATTIC

Memory is an attic where we store
    remnants of each day's existence--
Bits and pieces of experience,
    of love and things enjoyed,
    a child's silver laughter,
    a mother's whispered prayer,
    a lover's gentle touch;
    the sweet content of friendship shared
    and friendship lost restored;
    accomplishments that brought delight
    and sense of deep reward;
And places visited with hearts agape
    and wondering eyes at scenes
    too beautiful for words;
And times when God stooped low
    or we reached high
    to feel his presence near.

Memory is an attic where we go
    to reminisce--And find our
    hoarded treasures grown dim
    with attic dust--the speck by speck
    patina of nostalgia softening the lines
    of neatly bundled packages
    grown mellow with the years.

And 'mid those stored up treasures
    are some that bear the mark
    of sorrow's passing shadow
    and grief's deep rending wounds;
The anguish of unrequited love,
    of loneliness and emptiness of spirit
    that the heart somehow refused
    to give up to oblivion
    but kept there with the rest--
Bits and pieces of ourselves,
    too dear to cast away.

We marvel at their presence there,
And yet we somehow know
    that sorrow often taught us,
    and sadness made us grow
    more prone to be forgiving,
    less quick to take offense--
And grief was recompensed by love.

FRIENDSHIP LASTS

When I consider how
the miles   and   the years
have intervened to deny the joy
    of hands that touch in greeting
    and smiles that mark a pleasure shared,
I weep--   and   the tears
        stain the page on which I write.

But as I reminisce
    I know you've been there all along,
    rejoicing in our common joys
    and weeping at our common pain.

For friends who once have shared
    both joy   and   pain
        never lose the oneness
        that unites their hearts.
And friendship lasts despite
    the miles   and   the years.

THE DAYS OF OUR YEARS

The days of our years will fade
    to memories that cheer
    or load our hearts with grief.

And the residue of laughter and of tears
    has a taste that's bitter sweet.

Shun not the pain; receive it as God's gift;
    for victory implies a foe,
        and sorrow accents joy!

THE TWINKLE OUT OF STARS

And now they want to take
        the twinkle out of stars
with telescopes that see
        right through the haze that
        makes them scintillate.

But footprints on the moon
        didn't kill romance or
change the magic landscape
        bathed in moon's soft light.

And stars deprived of infinitesimal
        bits of mystery
will still twinkle when at night
        I walk beneath
        the studded canopy of sky.

THE TREES SEEMED TALLER

The trees seemed taller then,
    and the farm where childhood days
    were spent between the fenced-in yard
        and roaming with my dog
    a huge expanse of fields and woods
        of oak and pine, and hills, steep-sided,
        where the rock outcropped
        in ledges and miniature caves.

There I learned to love the moss that grew
    in crevices of rock, and arbutus'
    trailing vines and pink-white flowers
        that filled the woods with fragrance;
    and I knew where lady's slippers marked
    the acid soil, and princess pine
        graced the forest floor.

But now the farm has shrunk in size,
    and trees that in a small boy's eyes
    took giant strides across the hills
        don't nearly reach the sky.

The trees seemed taller then,
    but now my heart has grown, and the awe
    evoked by all that sprang from loamy soil
        embraces stars as well as moss
        and woodland flowers.

WRAPPED IN CLAY

I was born of the earth the day
    when God stooped down
    and from the clay
Made muddy forms and into one
    breathed the breath
    which up to then
    was his alone,
And I became his image!

    I am of earth--
    Of earth I'll be
    Even as I bear the mark
    of him who breathed
    his life in me.

Now, as I live, this task I own,
    To love the earth
    as I love God,
Acknowledging
    My need of both,
    wrapped in clay
And divinity.

A LIVING WEB

I am part of a living web
    Ordained at the dawn of time,
A web that is vibrant with music,
    Complete with meter and rhyme.

And the river of life that sustains me,
    That I feel pulsing inside,
Is deep as the deepest ocean,
    And wide as the world is wide.

TOMORROW IS TODAY REPEATED

Sometimes I think the calendar
    was made by those
Who've had a falling out with life
    and want it finished,
Or at least to hasten on to days
    of brighter prospect.

But *tomorrow* is just a name we give
    for today repeated,
Except for those who've schemed and planned,
    and added toil
To make their dreams worth waiting for.
    But such as these
Enjoy today too much to wish
    their life away.

A FACE THAT'S GONE

As the parched earth
    groans with internal stress
    when clouds clear
Yielding not the blessed rain,

So my heart years
    for an unheard voice
    and a face that's gone,
Nor comes again.

A PRISONER OF THE DARK

The daytime world teems with life
    In forest and field and in the air;
My world is wide and unrestrained,
    I walk with freedom everywhere.

But when the sun has left the sky
    And stars shine forth with meager light,
Another world begins to stir
    Beyond the limits of my sight.
Nocturnal creatures roam the fields,
    And night birds call from distant trees,
Or sail the sky in search of prey,
    And musky smells float on the breeze.

    I try in vain with daytime eyes,
    And ears alert, and hungry heart,
    To pierce the pall that shuts me in,
    A helpless prisoner of the dark.

THE BACK ROADS OF LIFE

I've gone by jet and diesel train,
I've travelled the seas and broad highways;
I've hurried here, I've hurried there,
    pushed and pulled by need and care.

    But the best of what I cherish now
    I've learned as I travelled
        the back roads of life.

I've countless memories that enrich my life,
Of things I've seen and things I've done,
Of joys I've known and sorrows shared,
    and moments with people who've
        loved and cared.

    The fondest hope I cherish now--
    To spend more time
        on the back roads of life.

EYES OPEN DREAMS

Dreams that come in fitful sleep
    Flee when dawn's first streaks of light
Push back the curtains that have veiled
    The daytime from the night.

And dreams that steal the waking hours
    From useful thought within the mind,
Build castles in the clouds of air
    That vanish with the wind.

But dreams we dream with open eyes
    Become the plan by which we build
The citadels of thought and deed
    That rise to bless the world.

"I SEE THY CROSS,
THERE TEACH MY HEART TO CLING."*

The trouble with clinging to a cross is that
    someone will put a crown of thorns
        on your head,
    or run a spear into your side.
This should not be cause for grave concern,
    for Christians should be willing
    to be hurt for the gospel's sake.
And yet, it is more than being willing;
    it is a matter of putting one's self daily
    in the way of being hurt.
For it is the nature of the world,
    that if one is faithful to the gospel,
    hurt will come.
And it is of the nature of the kingdom
    that the one who dies
    for the gospel's sake
        will be raised to life.

From the hymn "Spirit of God, Descend Upon My Heart,"
    by George Croly.

MY WALK WITH GOD

Beside the lake
of emerald green
with restless waves
tossed by the wind
My lakeside walk
is close with God.

Across the fields
of prairie grass
with daisies bright
and roses wild
My sunlit walk
is close with God.

Beneath the trees
where ferns combine
with adder's tongue
and columbine
My woodland walk
is close with God.

And when at night
I walk alone
'neath arching trees
or star filled skies
My silent walk
is close with God.

In winter white
or summer green
or bloom of spring
or gold of fall,
My Green Lake walk
is close with God.

In studied word and fervent prayer
with others shared whom God has called
to press the daily kingdom task
My daily walk is close with God.

SO LET ME WALK

He walked with God--
    across the hills
    beside the sea
    through village streets
    of Galilee,
    sometimes alone
    or in company
when Christ enfleshed divinity.

He walked with God--
    found hope restored,
    felt soul renewed
    and flesh made strong,
    by Galilee
    he healed the sick
    and stilled the sea
when Christ enfleshed divinity.

So let my walk
    be close to God
    with seeking heart
    beside the silent
    inland sea,
    that I may walk
    where'er he walks
with those whose need God's given me.

IN MY SEARCH TO KNOW

In my childhood search to know I probed
    the nooks and crannies of my world
    and learned that orioles weave their nests
    with skill that defies the force
    of tree-tops tossed by storms;
    that milk comes from grass transformed
    by cows I drove to pasture.

And at school I learned of two and four,
    and words that came from Greek and Latin
    and all the tongues of people's
    'round the world.

And when I finished I scarce was done,
    for new adventure waited, and still awaits,
    if I would understand and use
    the knowledge that's to be gained
    in such a way as to bless the world.

WHEN FAITH DISPELS THE GLOOM

Placed in the balance --

>> Hope and Despair
>> Belief and Doubt
>> Joy and Sorrow
>> Ease and Pain

-- the negative, with leaden density,
>> o'er weighs the plus of life
>>> and turns the devil's trick
>>> to triumph over good.

Hard it is to laugh,
>> when the breast conceals
>>> an aching heart!

Except when Faith dispels the gloom;
>> Then midnight seems as dawn.

TRUTH GROWS OUT OF TRUTH

No generation ever held
    its truth to be the same
        as for the generation past.

And if you search the sacred text,
    which story do you hold,
        the first one or the last?

The marvel is not that Truth,
    once revealed, is ended
        when the book is closed.

We read again the ancient words
    and in our search
        often find new meaning.

Truth grows out of Truth
    as new occasions make demand
        commensurate with the times.

DRY BONES LIVE

When spirit flees and flesh decays
    and sinews drop in withered shreds
    from bones that dry and whiten in the sun,
       till valley walls return the sound of
       rattling bones that spell a morbid
          tale of death . . .
All hope is lost - - -
       except God speak the word of life again.

Until God breathes the spirit new
    and sinews mend, and flesh restored
       gives shape and form,
    and spirit fills the hollow corpse
         there is no life.

But God can fill the bleaching bones
    with vital breath, until, reborn,
    dry bones rise to lives of praise again.

HEAVEN'S NOT EMPIRICAL

When poets rhyme
of future time
In language often lyrical

And skeptics scoff
"One world's enough"
In phrases sharp, satirical

And cynic smirks
at Godly works
And any kind of miracle

The truth lies not
in either/or
For heaven's not empirical.

BEYOND OUR DUE

Along the river, boulder strewn,
    and through the rock filled woods
I searched for quarry undefined
    by shape or name or kind.

Some lovely thing--a mossy bank,
    or multi-colored bow from
Sun-touched spray flung up by force
    of river's stemless flow;
A songbird calling for its mate,
    or lovely woodland flower.

And there it was among the rocks!
    A painted trillium prized
    as much for being rare
    as for its being delicate and fair.

And then I thought of you, dear friend,
    and knew the parable,
That friendship is a gift from God
    beyond our due.

PRAYER OF AN ECOLOGIST

Father, you gave us a garden,
    and we ate forbidden fruit.

You gave us knowledge to sail the oceans,
    and we found a continent, which we
    called "new" because "we" had not
        been here before.
We massacred the people, because
    they were not our kind.
We called it ours, although it had been
    their home for centuries.
We slaughtered the bear and bison;
We destroyed the forest that had grown
    for a thousand years;
We stripped the land of coal and minerals;
We put the plow to the prairie
    and squandered its topsoil
    so that half of a dozen states
    now muddies the Mississippi and
        forms its delta.
To cover our sins we soak the soil
    with chemicals that pollute our wells
    and contaminate our food.

We repent of our sins;
We ask forgiveness
        and for wisdom to become
        good stewards of your world,
Joining with you in processes that make
        for health;
Preserving for future generations
        the earth with its beauty and ability
        to nurture all that you created.

Bless us for the task to which we set
        our hands, and give us the will
        to see it through.

LISTEN TO THE LAND

Listen to the Land! Let it speak
    in ancient accents
    before the dawn of time,
    when all was dark and formless
    and God had drawn the lines
    that limited the oceans
    and thrust the mountains up--
Listen to the Land! Let it speak
    of seas and islands,
    of creatures of the deep,
    and creeping things and flying things,
    and days for work and nights for sleep,
    and sun and moon for seasons,
    and stars to deck the sky--

Listen to the Land! Let it speak
    of sharp uplifted mountains,
    and ancient inland seas,
    and ice that flowed like rivers
    across the valleys and the hills,
    of forests dark with shadows,
    and prairies rich with grass--
When God reviewed creation
    and declared that it was good.

Listen to the Land! and hear
    its agonizing cry
        fo᠆ rivers running dark with mud;
and creatures robbed of habitat;
        and trees that burn as if on pyres
        for the funeral of the world.

Listen to the Land! and weep
        that children yet unborn
        may never wake to robin's song,
        or know the shade of trees
        or fragrance of a rose.

Listen to the Land! and hear
        within the primal garden
        the voice of One who said:
        "Care for it . . . or die!"

KID GLOVES AND NO SOCKS

Miss Carrie had class,
    Miss Carrie had style.
Whenever she passed
    People stopped for a while
To admire this lady,
    Demure and neat,
From carefully coiffed hair
    To button-shoed feet.

Her stiffly starched collar,
    With ruffles and lace,
Enhanced the beauty of rouge
    spotted face;
Her corsetted bodice,
    Slender and round,
And full flowing skirt
    That reached to the ground.

But out in the street,
Avoiding puddles of rain,
Or mounting the stairs,
Ascendance to gain,
A stark revelation
Her pretenses mocked--
Her uplifted skirts
Revealed no socks.

"Kid gloves and no socks;
Kid gloves and no socks,"
With merciless glee
The children all mocked.

"Kid gloves and no socks;
Kid gloves and no socks,"
With merciless glee
Her pretense they mocked.

From a childhood memory of a story my grandmother
used to tell.--lhj

INDEX OF POEMS